let's travel in
SWITZERLAND

Edited by Darlene Geis

A TRAVEL PRESS BOOK

PICTURE ACKNOWLEDGMENTS

The full-color pictures and illustrations in this book are the work of the following photographers and artists, whose collaboration is gratefully acknowledged.

Werner Lüthy, from P.I.P. (1, 2, 3, 6, 7, 10, 14, 15, 16, 17, 18, 19, 21, 22, 23, 24, 26, 27, 28, 29, 30, 31, 32): Guy Auvert, from P.I.P. (4, 25); Tom Hollyman, from Photo Researchers (5); Photo Giegel from P.I.P. (8, 11); Fritz Henle, from Photo Researchers (9, 12, 13); the Swiss Cheese Council (20). For the black-and-white photographs we wish to thank the Swiss National Tourist Office and Werner Lüthy, from P.I.P. The map was made by Enrico Arno. Book designed by Mann Associates.

CONTENTS

FRANCE

GER

Basel **4**

Rhine River

24

Aare River

Zurich **11**

L. of Zurich

JURA MOUNTAINS

31

L. of Neuchâtel

21

23

Lucerne **26**

L. Lucerne

13-17
Bern

Emme River

27

25

Fribourg

L. of Thun **10**

19

20

5

Lausanne

7

EIGER
MÖNCH

6

Rivaz
28

JUNGFRAU

1

30
Castle of Chillon

THE

29
Geneva

Rhone River

Simplon Tunnel

MATTERHORN

FRANCE

32 **2**
Zermatt

L. Maggiore

Great St. Bernard Pass

I

T

Locales of thirty-two full-page pictures

SWITZERLAND, HOLIDAY PARADISE

PERCHED like a picturesque fortress on the roof of Europe, tiny Switzerland enjoys a peaceful and industrious life behind its mountain bastions. The frontiers of five countries—France, Italy, Austria, Germany and Liechtenstein—surround this land of green valleys and snow-clad peaks, but it has remained an island of neutrality in the midst of the wars that have swirled around it during the past century. Unscarred by battles, unblemished by the poverty that is often war's aftermath, Switzerland offers the traveler the charm of neat cities and villages and the unflawed grandeur of its mountain scenery.

In a country of only 16,000 square miles—less than half the size of our state of Maine—you will find everything from pine forests to palm trees, icy glaciers and mild blue lakes, quiet streams and thundering waterfalls, smooth meadows and towering peaks, ancient castles and soaring modern bridges. Switzerland is a vacationer's paradise because of this fascinating variety crammed into so small an area.

The country is divided into three main regions: the Alps to the south, the Swiss plateau in the center, and the Jura (JOOR-*ah*), a chain of low, forested mountains that curves from west to north. But overlying these three regions is a crazy quilt of hills and valleys, rivers and lakes that breaks Switzerland up into hundreds of tiny locales, each with its own special atmosphere and charm.

When a Swiss says he loves his country, he is probably not speaking of Switzerland as a whole—he means his own canton or district, or even the little valley, ringed with familiar mountains, that is his home. No two of these valleys are alike, and the inhabitants of one are apt to refer to the people of the next village as "foreigners." Yet, for all their differences, the Swiss are bound together in a firm confederation whose motto is *One for All and All for One.*

LAND OF FOUR LANGUAGES

There is not even one common language in this small country. Out of every hundred Swiss, seventy-two speak German as their mother tongue, twenty-one speak French, six speak Italian, and one clings to an ancient Latin dialect called Romansh (*roh*-MANSH). Aside from a main language, nearly everyone in Switzerland speaks at least one other, but with a definite Swiss accent. Among themselves their mispronunciations are a source of great amusement.

The stubborn resistance to a common language is indicative of the love of independence and fierce individuality that are so striking a part of the national character. This land that is at the crossroads of Europe was desirable to many peoples—Celtic, Germanic and Burgundian tribes settled here; Attila, Vercingetorix (*vuhr-sin*-JET-*uh-rix*) and Julius Caesar marched this way. But the mountains kept the various groups separated, and each district has jealously guarded its individuality ever since.

BIRTHPLACE OF HEROES

In Switzerland, the elemental forces of nature created a wild and rugged country where massive peaks loom forbiddingly over narrow valleys. Only a hardy breed of men could have wrested a livelihood from this mountain wilderness and survived through the centuries to tame it and create the playground of pleasure that Switzerland is now.

William Tell is the most famous national hero, and though his story has become a blend of legend and fact, it is true to the courage and love of freedom characteristic of the Swiss. Tell may have shot the apple off his son's head on orders from an Austrian tyrant whom he later killed. And he may well have been one of the men who took part in the uprising at the Rütli (REWT-*lee*) Meadow, where representatives of three of the Forest Cantons swore to unite against their Austrian oppressors. In any case, William Tell symbolizes the strong, rough foresters whose pact of mutual assistance on August 1, 1291, was the cornerstone of the

Swiss Confederation, which now includes twenty-two cantons.

Some years later, in 1315, an Austrian army, 20,000 strong, marched on the Forest Canton of Schwyz (SHVEETS), which gave its name to Switzerland. The young federation of cantons rounded up a band of 1300 determined men who defended themselves by sending an avalanche of boulders and tree trunks crashing down on the Austrian forces in the pass below. The stunning victory of crudely armed peasants over the flashing troops of knights in armor attracted other towns and districts to the league—each eager to protect itself without forfeiting its independence.

By the sixteenth century the Confederation had become a major military power with a membership of thirteen cantons. The hardy men who had learned to fight in self-defense now took up arms as a profession, and Swiss mercenaries won glory in other countries. The famous Swiss Guard of the Vatican has defended the popes for four hundred years. And the kings of France, who could afford the best, employed Swiss mercenaries to watch over them. Eight hundred of Louis XVI's Swiss Guards were slaughtered by the Paris mob when they tried to defend the royal family during the Revolution. Their monument, the noble statue of the Wounded Lion of Lucerne (*loo*-SURN), is one of the showplaces of that city, commemorating the loyalty and valor of Swiss men-at-arms.

William Tell lives in his countrymen's hearts and in the yearly festival where his deeds are re-enacted.

PEACEFUL SANCTUARY

Though Swiss soldiers hired out to fight the battles of other countries, their own country's interests and sympathies were so diverse that Switzerland as a nation was never able to take sides in any of the continental wars that raged around it. Other nations were grateful to have this country, the guardian of mountain passes that are gateways from one part of Europe to another, remain in its lofty and disinterested role of neutral.

As a neutral country Switzerland opened its doors to refugees and political exiles from all nations. But perhaps even more important, this land of awe-inspiring beauty became a sanctuary for great numbers of travelers who refreshed themselves in the bracing mountain air and found that a vacation in Switzerland gave them renewed vitality for the months to come. Over the years, artists and thinkers too have sought inspiration here. There is one inn at Zurich (ZOOR-*ick*) whose guest book includes the names of Goethe (GUH-*teh*), Victor Hugo, Alexandre Dumas (*dew*-MAH), Schlegel (SHLEH-*gehl*), Mozart, Liszt, Brahms and a glittering assortment of kings and emperors. But though foreign artists have thrived in the creative climate of Switzerland, few of her native sons have excelled in the arts.

CHEESE, WATCHES AND DDT

A character in the movie *The Third Man* observed, "Switzerland has lived in peace for three centuries, and what has she given us? The cuckoo clock." It is true that no world-shaking artistic or scientific talent has sprung from the peaceful soil of Switzerland. But as practitioners of the

Bridges span deep valleys and a network of railways now unites the Swiss cantons.

minor arts—wood-carving, embroidery, painted furniture—and as meticulous craftsmen, the Swiss excel, and they have given the world a wide variety of quality products.

Originally Switzerland was a country of farmers and herdsmen. Today, less than one-fifth of the population is engaged in agriculture. But the herds of sleek cattle grazing in lush mountain meadows are still one of the important sources of Swiss income. Dairy products made from their rich milk are exported to numerous countries where Swiss cheese and Swiss chocolate carry the good wholesome flavor of Switzerland to people far beyond its borders.

Switzerland is probably most famous for its watches, considered by many to be the best in the world. The Swiss are sadly lacking in raw materials, but they have learned to compensate for that lack by the superior quality of their workmanship. A watch is tiny and uses very little material. It is the precision of its infinitesimal parts that makes it tick, and Swiss watches tick better than any others. Today watches, precision instruments and machinery account for nearly 50 per cent of Swiss exports.

The painstaking perfectionism of the Swiss—that quality that gives each city and village its immaculate charm—has enabled the small country to hold its own in world markets. Swiss chemicals and drugs, too, are used all over the world. Switzerland pioneered in the careful research that led to the industrial production of DDT, the highly successful insecticide. Pharmaceuticals are now Switzerland's third largest export.

HOSTS AND BANKERS TO THE WORLD

The traveler in Switzerland may not be aware of its industrial strength. Factories are small and dispersed throughout the country, and there are no ugly industrialized centers. But the quality and quantity of Swiss hotels cannot long escape one's notice.

Switzerland plays host to nearly four million paying guests a year, and the enormous tourist revenue from the "invisible exports" of holiday fun helps make up the country's deficit between real exports and imports. The Swiss franc (worth about 23 cents) is so solid and stable that its value has remained virtually the same for thirty years—a remarkable feat in these days of roller-coaster fluctuations in foreign currencies.

This economic stability, coupled with Switzerland's location at the heart of Europe (and aided, no doubt, by those strong, safe walls of mountains) has contributed to the country's importance as a banking center. There is one bank for every 1300 Swiss inhabitants, the highest proportion in the world. And Switzerland can boast that it has more savings accounts than people. Not only are its own citizens frugal, but a great many foreigners also like to keep money in the security of Swiss banks, often in secret accounts.

THE INTERNATIONAL NATION

Swiss capital, in the form of loans and credits, has been invested in numerous foreign countries, giving Switzerland a stake in their development and well-being. And many Swiss industries have foreign branches or affiliates, all of which add to the international point of view practiced by this small country.

Switzerland is the birthplace of the International Red Cross, founded originally to give care and protection to war casualties. The Geneva Convention—a code of rules governing treatment of prisoners of war—grew out of the first international conference in Geneva. There the Swiss flag, a white cross on a red ground, was reversed and the Red Cross became both the emblem and the name for the international agency.

Switzerland is also the home of the Universal Postal Union, the World Bank, the International Labor Office, and the Bern Convention which sets down the rules for international copyright. The League of Nations used to be based in Geneva, and its Palace of Nations now houses European offices for the United Nations. International institutions flourish in Switzerland, bringing the country into contact with delegates from five continents. Many of them see in Switzerland far more than a country of breath-taking picture-postcard views. They see instead that Switzerland is in miniature what Europe—or even the whole world— might one day be. Here, in a setting of unbelievable splendor, are people of different backgrounds and different religions, speaking different languages yet living in harmonious union.

The time when canton fought bitterly against canton is long past, though faint echoes of the old bitterness can sometimes be heard in the Federal Assembly. But most of all the visitor hears the sweet sounds of peace in the land, the gentle clanking of cowbells, a splashing waterfall, the deep notes of the alpenhorn echoing from mountain to mountain. The world seems good and beautiful in Switzerland—and that, perhaps, is why travelers have thronged here for centuries. Faced with the majesty of nature, who does not come away a little better than he was before?

This glorious playground of sparkling lakes and cloud-capped mountains delights its citizens and visitors alike.

let's travel in

SWITZERLAND

ALPINE MEADOW: THE BERNESE OBERLAND

I F YOU could choose only one of Switzerland's twenty-two cantons to visit, you would probably choose Bern (BURN), the second largest. Cutting through the country from the French border almost to the Italian, Bern contains a slice of the Jura, a section of the Swiss plain, and a wedge of the Oberland, or highlands, that rise to the snow-covered Alps.

The red-roofed city of Bern, capital of the Swiss Confederation, is in this canton, and Interlaken (IN-*ter-lah-ken*), an elegant resort, stands between two long blue lakes. Nearby rises one of the most famous peaks in Switzerland, the icy Jungfrau (YOONG-*frow*), or Maiden, cloaked in white. But the great charm of this district is in its southern section—the Bernese Oberland—which manages somehow to combine the pastoral with the spectacular. We see it here in this meadow, whose grassy hill is spangled with Alpine wildflowers. Trees seem to march up the steep slopes, and rustic cabins cling to the hillsides. In the blue distance, rocky peaks scrape the clouds, and their snow-streaked flanks make a boldly dramatic background for the pleasant meadow.

In the late spring, villagers climb from their snug houses in the valleys below to these upland fields, driving their cattle to summer pastures. This is called the *inalpe,* the occasion when cows are freed from winter stables to fatten on upland meadows. The villagers remain in these rough mountain huts for a few weeks. Then, when the full glory of summer warms the land, young boys take the cows to even higher pastures. You can see them grazing 8000 feet up, and in the clear, thin air the distant music of their cowbells carries across the valley. Meanwhile the men, women and children of the village must cut and gather enough hay from these fields to feed their cows during the bitter winter to come. The land is beautiful, but it exacts a harsh price in toil.

16

VILLAGE OF
ZERMATT:
AT THE FOOT OF
THE MATTERHORN

A TOY village of wooden chalets (*sha*-LAZE) clustered on an emerald lawn— that is Zermatt (*tsehr*-MAHT), one of the most picturesque resorts in Switzerland. Dwarfing the village is the white spear point of the Matterhorn, stabbing the sky at an altitude of 14,780 feet. This angular peak has cast a powerful spell over mountain climbers for centuries, luring many to their death with its majestic challenge. The Matterhorn was finally conquered in 1865 by an Englishman named Edward Whymper, but even after the victory, four members of Whymper's party were killed on the descent. It is said that when Queen Victoria heard of her subject's feat she turned to her ministers and demanded whether such stupidity ought not to be forbidden.

Nowadays hundreds of mountaineers climb the Matterhorn each year under the expert leadership of Zermatt's guides. Members of the Swiss Alpine Club, these guides have been given a long and thorough training in the science of Alpinism, and they have a great fund of practical experience. In Zermatt, the guides will tell you that any four of them can get a cow up to the very summit of the Matterhorn. It is possible that Swiss cows have, of necessity, more mountain-climbing know-how than many tourists.

Zermatt, for all its miniature prettiness, is really a town for the tough-fibered. It has long been the mountaineering capital of Switzerland. Now, one of Switzerland's most remarkable railways twists and climbs through the mountains to Zermatt's plateau. If you are not a do-it-yourself mountaineer, the train will also carry you from Zermatt to the Gorner Grat (GOR-*ner* GRAHT). There, at an altitude of over 10,000 feet, you will be in the awesome company of the Alpine giants, gazing at a panorama of glaciers and peaks that was once the privilege of the daring few.

18

SHEEP-SHEARING: CANTON OF THE GREY LEAGUES

LIFE for the country people of Switzerland has none of the holiday glamour that tourists enjoy. And in the canton of the Gray Leagues—known also as the Grisons (*gree*-ZOHN) in French, or Graubünden (GRAH-*oo-bewn-den*) in German—you find a region that is wild and harsh and in many places still quite primitive. The largest of the Swiss cantons, this one is the most sparsely populated because of its rugged and fierce terrain. And its people have been stubbornly independent. One-third of its population still speaks the archaic language Romansh, handed down from Roman forebears.

The Gray Leagues did not join the Swiss Confederation until 1803. Long after railways were built in the rest of Switzerland, they refused to permit them to cross their borders. Until 1927 automobiles were barred from the canton's roads—unless they were horse-drawn! But modern times and the lure of tourist wealth finally won out.

Now some of the most fashionable Swiss resorts are to be found in the Grisons—St.-Moritz (*sant moh-*RITZ), Klosters (KLOHS-*tehrs*), Davos (*dah*-VOHSS), Arosa (*ah*-ROH-*zah*)— and there is an undreamed-of prosperity in those tourist centers. The natives like to joke that the main business of the Grisons is "the Germans, the English, cattle and wood." But in the remote valleys, people and livestock still share huts like this one, wool comes from one's own sheep, and the glittering world of pleasure could be on another planet.

Nylon—a far cry from the homespun of rural villages—is produced in up-to-date factories.

OLD BASEL: CITY ON THE RHINE

WE TEND to think of Switzerland as a country of rural villages and picturesque resorts, forgetting that it is strung with a band of cities, five of which have populations of over a hundred thousand. Basel (BAH-*zel*) is one of the oldest Swiss cities, and after Zurich it is the largest. In the year 44, the Romans built a fortification on the Rhine called Basilia. It became the city of Basel, which spans the river near the point where the French, German and Swiss frontiers meet. Basel is a commercial city, but in Switzerland charm and commerce are not incompatible. So we find shops and business houses situated in fine old buildings, and many firms display their name and product on handsome wrought-iron signs that are decorative rather than blatant.

Although it is a landlocked country, Switzerland has important rivers linking it with four seas. Here at Basel, five million tons of merchandise are handled each year on the quays that line the river. Ships sail from this inland port down the Rhine through Germany and Holland to the North Sea. Jokes about the Swiss Navy have gone out of style, for Switzerland now has an efficient Merchant Marine totaling 200,000 tons, with ocean-going vessels that sail proudly under the white cross of the Swiss flag.

A fleet of 120 steamers sails Switzerland's lakes, and it is even possible to enter the country by boat.

CITIZEN SOLDIER: ETERNAL VIGILANCE

THE price of freedom and the long peace Switzerland has enjoyed are exemplified by the man in this picture. He and every healthy Swiss male between the ages of twenty and sixty must be both citizen and soldier. "Switzerland does not *have* an army, Switzerland *is* an army!" explained one of her military leaders. When a young man is in his twentieth year he must spend seventeen weeks in recruit school. If physical defects bar him from army service he will pay an additional tax each year until he is forty-eight.

The soldiers graduate from their training as privates, and each one is given a rifle, twenty-four rounds of ammunition, and any specialized equipment his army job requires. These he takes *home* with him—and if you stop to think about it, there are few governments in the world today who could trust their citizens with home arsenals! It is every man's duty to keep his equipment and uniform constantly ready for use, and the citizen in this picture is cleaning his rifle while enjoying the view of his peaceful valley high in the Bernese Oberland.

The tradition of William Tell's deadly marksmanship lives on in the Swiss today. Riflery is a national sport, and shooting matches on Saturdays serve the double purpose of keeping marksmanship up to scratch, and allowing the rivalries between cantons to have a sporting outlet. The citizen soldiers must pass frequent marksmanship tests, and they have regular refresher courses in military training until they are forty-eight years old, though the men are subject to call until they are sixty.

Switzerland, with her army always at the ready, can mobilize 600,000 citizens in three days. She is, on a per capita basis, the most heavily armed nation in the world. She is also prepared, in case of imminent attack, to blow up her tunnels, block the mountain passes and destroy strategic bridges, trusting the impassable Alpine terrain to discourage invaders.

ALPINE MOUNTAINEERS: SCALING THE MONCH

THE mountains that guard Switzerland's peace so well might be invincible to armies, but generations of mountaineers have devoted themselves to the conquest of individual peaks. Climbing has become more than a sport—it is a cult and a science, and its practitioners consider the Swiss Alps their most challenging proving ground.

These are not the highest mountains in the world, nor are they necessarily the most difficult—though there are some peaks that have yet to surrender to the mountaineers' strategy and skill. But the Alps offer an exciting variety of climbs—over glaciers that are like frozen seas of blue-white ice, on rock formations that take striking architectural shapes with towers, pinnacles, turrets and vaulted arches testing the ingenuity of the climber and rewarding him with scenes of unbelievable magnificence.

Here we see a guide and climber, roped together and making the

The funicular at Niesen climbs to 7600 feet for spectacular views of the Bernese Alps.

difficult ascent of the Mönch (MUNSH). Three mighty peaks, all over 13,000 feet high, stand side by side. The Eiger (EYE-*gher*), the Mönch and the Jungfrau—Ogre, Monk and Maiden—like wicked monsters in a fairy tale, have taken their toll of victims. But all have succumbed at last to climbers who have reached their summits in triumph. In fact, the Swiss Alpine Club guidebook now gives eighty-one possible routes for scaling the Jungfrau.

SKY TRAIN: CABLE CAR ON THE RINDERBERG

FORTUNATELY for many of of us, Switzerland has provided another easier way to get to the top of some of her mountains. Electricity takes the place of muscle, nerve, ice ax and rope, enabling thousands of people who would otherwise never have made the grade to stand triumphantly halfway between heaven and earth.

Here on the Rinderberg, with only the tops of neighboring Alps visible above the clouds, an aerial cable car carries passengers up the snowy slope. In summer the cable cars or chair lifts are used by sight-seers. In winter they do the uphill climb for skiers, who clamber out of the mechanical chrysalis when it reaches the summit and then wing their way downwards over the trackless snow.

The Swiss aerial railways are remarkable engineering feats. Some of them are strung up mountain slopes like this one, some are hung across deep valleys with a little car suspended from a slender cable in the middle of nowhere. Actually, the entire railway system of Switzerland is wonderful. The country's one great natural resource is water power, cascading from the countless rivers and falls that ornament the landscape. Hydroelectric power runs the country, and 98 per cent of Swiss trains are electrified.

The Federal Railways are clean, efficient and inexpensive. They wind around valleys, cut through mountains, cross fantastic bridges, and your destination becomes unimportant compared with the delight of getting there. The trains have three classes of accommodations, but the frugal Swiss generally travel third class. A top government councilor was recognized once in a third-class coach. "Sir, why do you travel third class?" he was asked. The councilor answered brusquely, "Because there is no fourth class."

LUXURIOUS
ST.-MORITZ:
ENGADINE
RESORT

FOR first-class, de luxe, all-out luxury, there are few places in the world to equal St.-Moritz. This spa nestles between the mountains of the Upper Engadine (EN-*gah-deen*), as the valley of the Inn River is called, on the shores of a sapphire lake. St.-Moritz is really three little villages strung together by roads. The highest one, St.-Moritz Dorf, is the gathering place for international society, and was the first of the winter-sports resorts. Here, when the lake is frozen to an icy blue and the mountains sparkle whitely —when pine trees are dusted with snow and the air at 6000 feet is like a fine, dry wine—the wealthy, the titled, the powerful gather for their winter holiday. St.-Moritz has played host to serious athletes, too. It has been the scene of several Olympic competitions.

The hotels are palatial and look imposing even against their backdrop of looming mountains. At night they glitter with lights like huge ships sailing on a sea of snow. And they are expensive! But there are smaller inns and guesthouses where travelers can stay in comfort and still enjoy the skiing, skating, bobsledding or climbing as much as any millionaire.

St.-Moritz Bad (BAHD), which we see here, is on slightly lower ground where the Inn River empties into the Lake of St.-Moritz. Switzerland is renowned for its health resorts, and there are three mineral springs in this village that have given it the name *Bad,* or Bath. For 3000 years people have come to drink and bathe in the curative waters that bubble up from beneath the mountain masses, bearing a gift of health-giving minerals. Although medicine has come a long way in 3000 years, there are few new discoveries that can compare in therapeutic value with a holiday in a Swiss mountain village set in a sun-drenched valley.

FESTIVE
COSTUMES:
GIRLS
OF TARASP

AS THE Inn River makes its way from the Alps to Austria, its valley becomes the Lower Engadine, dotted with charming old villages like Tarasp (*tah*-RASP). This is in the Canton of the Grisons, where many people still speak Romansh and carry on the traditional arts and crafts in their buildings, wood-carvings and costumes. In the twelfth-century Castle of Tarasp, on the hill beyond the village, there is a fascinating collection of historical folk art where the Swiss genius for decoration can be admired close to its source.

It is not surprising that the Swiss cantons, cherishing as they do every feature that distinguishes them from their neighbors, have each developed a distinctive costume. The ladies of Fribourg (*free*-BOOR) dress up in hats that look like glittering pincushions; the ladies of Appenzell, famous for their needlework, wear pleated coifs and collars that show off their elaborate embroidery; the women of Bern sport black lace bonnets; and in the Grisons, or Gray Leagues, as if to counteract the

canton's drab name, the girls dress in bright, holly red. Early in this century the custom of wearing these colorful costumes began to die out. Then the National Costumes' League revived interest in these beautiful folk fashions. Now thousands of men and women dress up on Sundays, holidays and for the regional and national festivals, giving us a chance to see the people of Switzerland in their marvelously varied finery.

The charm of Alpine blossoms inspires the embroidery and painted designs traditional in village crafts.

BOATING ON LAKE THUN: THE BERNESE RIVIERA

LAKE Thun (TOON) is sheltered from the north wind by the Lower Alps and set dramatically within the curving amphitheater of the High Alps. As a result, the climate is mild and the shores of this narrow lake blossom with sunny resorts. From the city of Thun at one tip of the lake to Interlaken at the other, it is only an eleven-mile stretch, and neat white steamers cruise back and forth all day and during the evening. The shore line is punctuated with the pointed turrets and round towers of castles that have stood guard here since the Middle Ages, lending enchantment to a scene of tranquil loveliness.

For twentieth-century vacationers who want exercise with their sightseeing there is an abundance of activities. There are mountains for climbing and golden curves of beach for swimming. And as you can see in this picture, the glassy blue surface of Lake Thun is perfect for

Lugano, near the Italian border, basks beneath southern palms.

sailing. At Hilterfingen (HILL-ter-fing-ghen), one of the lakeside resorts, the best sailing and water-skiing schools in Switzerland use what must be the most scenic schoolroom in the world.

Though Switzerland is most famous as a winter playground, it is an ideal year-round resort. It would be possible to come down from an Alpine ski holiday in April and start all over again with bathing suit and water skis on balmy Lake Thun.

34

ZURICH
RIVER FRONT:
COMMERCIAL
METROPOLIS

THE solid, hard-working, orderly Swiss character is best exemplified by Switzerland's largest city, Zurich. This metropolis, with a population of 425,000, is ancient but its appearance and tempo are modern. Broad avenues lined with trees invite promenaders, and the main shopping street, prosaically named Bahnhofstrasse (BAHN-*hohf-shtrahs-seh*), or Station Street, is a half-mile display of fine shops, substantial banks and office buildings. Zurich's wealth comes from its industries, but though it is a manufacturing center, the city is immaculate and neither dirt nor smoke smudges its clean, sharp outlines.

Even the Limmat (LIM-*maht*) River coursing through the heart of Zurich retains its freshness and clarity. Along the riverbanks old houses and guildhalls from another era have been refurbished and are now stately restaurants dedicated to the good living for which Zurich is renowned. But good living is not synonymous with high living, and Zurichers are a careful lot, taking their pleasures sedately and shutting down the town with a midnight curfew.

The old church steeples remind us that it was here in Zurich that the Reformation was begun in the sixteenth century by Ulrich Zwingli (TSVING-*lee*). He was the pastor of the cathedral whose twin spires you can see at the right. Zwingli preached impassioned sermons against certain practices of the Church of Rome—especially the sale of indulgences. Civil war broke out and Zwingli was killed in the battle which defeated the Protestants. But John Calvin continued to preach Protestantism in Geneva, and eventually the majority of the Swiss Confederates swung behind him. Since then each canton has worshiped as it wishes, and in some small parishes Catholics and Protestants take turns using the same church. The austere influence of the old Reformers is still felt in the cities where they preached, and to this day Zurich maintains an air of puritanism and seriousness, and cloaks its wealth in unostentatious solidity.

MONASTERY OF
ST. GALLEN:
LIBRARY
OF TREASURES

FREEDOM of worship and freedom of thought have had a long history in Switzerland, and men from other lands have found this a liberal climate in which to sow their ideas. Erasmus came from Rotterdam to teach in Basel; Calvin fled France to preach in Geneva; and early in the seventh century an Irish monk named Gallus left his native County Down and journeyed to this spot near Lake Constance where he preached Christianity.

After the death of St. Gallus, his abbey became a school, and in the ninth and tenth centuries it was one of the most famous universities in Europe. Those were the Dark Ages, when the lamps of learning flickered and all but went out. Yet in the Abbey at St. Gallen (*sant* GAHL-*en*) a library was founded where precious manuscripts of the Greek and Roman classics were preserved, and seventh-century Irish manuscripts, brought to Switzerland by the monk's disciples, were cherished.

In this picture we see the magnificent baroque room that was built in the sixteenth century to house the collection of rare books and manuscripts. Now there are 100,000 volumes and manuscripts, some of them exquisitely illuminated prayer books painted letter by letter in the Middle Ages. Visitors must wear felt slippers when they walk on the inlaid floors. One of the treasures they will see displayed is a Bible printed in Nuremberg in 1599, with text in twelve parallel columns—English, French, German, Italian, Spanish, Danish, Polish, Moravian, Greek, Latin, Hebrew and Syrian. This Polyglot Bible is aptly housed in a country whose interests range over all the world.

KNIGHT OF BERN:
ORNAMENT IN
THE CAPITAL

THE capital of Switzerland is a cheerful city whose ancient buildings and fountains are kept freshly painted, giving Bern's antiquity a modern gloss. It was founded in 1191 by the Duke of Zähringen (TSEH-*ring-ghen*), who lived in a nearby castle. The Duke went hunting one day and decided that he would name his new city after the first game he shot. Luckily he bagged a bear—imagine a town named Rabbit or Mountain Goat! The shaggy brown beast has been the emblem and mascot of Bern ever since, and you can see it on the knight's banner, while a cub, armed with a sword, hides behind him. The live bears who disport themselves in the famous Bear Pit are the city's favorite pets, and no visit to Bern is complete without a sight of these furry clowns.

Bern was built on a rocky cliff around which the River Aare (AH-*reh*) makes a swift-flowing loop. Originally the Aare was the frontier between the duchies of Burgundy and Alemania, and consequently Bern shares a French and German heritage. Its arcaded streets and the fountains topped with vividly colored statues, like this one, were borrowed from Italy, while the steep tile roofs are typically Swiss, designed as protection against heavy snows. In the past many foreign influences met and left their mark here, and today the foreign offices and legations of numerous countries keep this medieval-looking town in touch with the modern world.

Baby bears lap their milk and entertain the townspeople of Bern.

41

MECHANICAL CLOCK TOWER: LANDMARK OF BERN

THE tidy charm of Swiss cities was not achieved overnight or by accident. It is a combination of antique buildings that are kept in fresh repair, and new additions that carefully preserve the old spirit. In the central part of Bern a distinctive gray-green sandstone that matches the material of the Parliament Building must be used in all new construction. From springtime till autumn, window boxes filled with vivid red geraniums make neat accents of color along the streets. There is a special organization that sees to it that the balconies of Bern flower in unison, and in houses where people cannot afford to keep their window boxes blooming, the organization picks up the tab. These are the special touches, the extra details that add up to an entrancing whole.

It goes without saying that the streets and sidewalks are kept spot-

Bern, on a snowy night, is a Christmas-card city of frosty lights.

lessly clean, and for many amazed tourists, who believe that municipal cleanliness is next to impossible, this comes as the greatest novelty of all. The other great novelty in Bern is the quaint mechanical Clock Tower facing us here. Built into one of the old city gates, the clock puts on an amusing show every hour. A rooster crows, bears dance, and a clown shakes his fist at the clock above him. This routine has gone on millions of times— the clock has been working since 1530 and is still running well.

MODERN WATCH
FACTORY:
SWITZERLAND'S
PRIDE

PERFORMING clocks, cuckoo clocks, music boxes and other mechanical toys that are made to delight and amuse can be found in the shops of every Swiss city. But the national reputation for precision manufacturing rests firmly on one small product—the watch. A Swiss watch can be plain or fancy, self-winding, antimagnetic, with a calendar or an alarm built in, and it can cost anything from a pittance to a fortune. Whatever the price, you know you are buying a quality instrument, and the same watch will cost you about 50 per cent less in Switzerland than it does in any other country.

There are 50,000 people employed in the watchmaking industry and they produce 25,000,000 watches each year. The idea of a timepiece so small that it could be carried in a man's pocket was a brilliant innovation in the seventeenth century. A blacksmith named Daniel Jeanrichard (*zhawn-ree-*SHAHR), who lived in a village of the Jura, was asked to repair a watch that belonged to an English traveler. He not only fixed this rarity, but he learned from it how to make watches on his own, and as a result of his skill and ingenuity the people of his region have had a prosperous local industry ever since.

Watches are made in other parts of the country, too, but the Jura, just across the border from France, is the most famous watchmaking center. They say that the necessary skills can only be acquired after several generations, and the top artisans must be born into a family of watchmakers. It takes steady nerves to make a precision watch, and women seem to have the calm patience necessary for the more delicate operations. But the top watchmakers are old-timers who refuse to work on an assembly line and have special quarters where not more than two of them occupy a room. When you see the shop windows of Switzerland filled with thousands of watches, you are looking at the fruit of millions of exacting hours spent in quest of precision and perfection.

OUTDOOR SHOPPING: MARKET DAY IN BERN

STORES in Switzerland are filled with a wealth of quality merchandise impeccably displayed for the tourist. Besides watches and music boxes there are excellent cameras, typewriters, silks and embroidered cottons, and the gay wood carvings that catch the spirit of rustic Swiss humor. Bern has its share of sophisticated shops, as befits the capital of the Confederation, but it is also a city surrounded by rich farmlands, and on Tuesdays and Saturdays it becomes a market town.

Usually the flower-decked buildings of Bern look down on a quiet city, but on market days the large square and streets near the Federal Palace are the scene of lively activity. Outdoor stalls are set up under awnings and umbrellas, displaying an orderly array of fruits, vegetables, flowers, pastries and even local fabrics. Most of the vendors are women, but they tend to business quietly, and there is none of the brawling excitement or noisy haggling over wares that sometimes characterizes open-air markets in other places.

One of the most popular and successful forms of merchandising in Switzerland is the "rolling store." Pioneered by an energetic business-man named Gottlieb Duttweiler, this fleet of trucks carries food, clothing and fuel directly from producer to customer at greatly reduced prices. The trucks and a chain of branch stores are called Migros (ME-*gross*), short for *demigros* or half-wholesale, and their low prices have played a large part in keeping the cost of living down and holding the line on inflation in Switzerland. Thrifty housewives in remote villages welcome the Migros truck which brings market day to their very doorstep, but for a lavish variety of good things to eat, the old-fashioned outdoor market is still unsurpassed.

CONFECTION OF THE COUNTRY: SWISS CHOCOLATE

FOR anyone who thinks that a piece of chocolate candy is the same the world over, the dazzling array of chocolates in Switzerland is an eye-opener. In this picture we are watching the girls in the Tobler factory in Bern as they pack boxes with an assortment of brightly wrapped candies. Actually the colored foil gilds the lily, for the glossy brown chocolate needs no further adornment. There are a number of well-known Swiss manufacturers of this confection whose names are known all over the world— Nestlé, Suchard, and Lindt and Sprüngli have satisfied many a foreign sweet tooth.

Chocolate was introduced to Europe by the Spaniards, who brought it back from Mexico in the sixteenth century. Although many countries manufacture candy from the cocoa bean, Swiss chocolate takes high honors. Switzerland, while it doesn't make more of any product than others do, certainly makes the best of it. Cocoa beans are cleaned and roasted, and their kernels are then ground in stone mills, producing a chocolate liquid that is at least half cocoa butter. For sweet chocolate, sugar and additional cocoa butter are added, and the resulting paste is ground once more, and given additional processing. The fat content, the time and care spent in processing, and the amount of milk added for milk chocolate are all factors in the ultimate flavor and quality of the candy. It is here that the Swiss add their priceless ingredient —perfectionism.

The famous Swiss cheese travels down from mountain pastures like this—the first stage of more distant journeys.

APPENZELL HERDSMAN: COWBOY OF SWITZERLAND

SWISS dairy products owe their excellence to sleek brown cows like this one, a member of an old, old breed native to the Alps. Short, solid legs make these animals particularly well-suited to the mountain climbing they must do in order to get to pasture. And the herdsman has to be something of a mountaineer himself. Unlike American cowboys, he accompanies Bossy on foot, and his sturdy shoes will take him high above his valley each summer, so the hay near the village can be saved for winter forage.

Here in Appenzell, not far from the Austrian border, we see a part of Switzerland whose rustic charm is still unspoiled. The women sit in their sunlit doorways making the exquisite embroidery for which the canton is renowned. Unfortunately the fragile handwork is giving way to machine-made designs. Who can afford to spend months embroidering one delicate handkerchief or doily?

Sometimes the men wear their colorful costumes while they work. The early-summer climb to mountain pastures is a festive occasion for which they will surely dress in their yellow and scarlet best, with one gold earring adding a jaunty note. The herdsman will deck his broad-brimmed hat with flowers, and his cows will wear garlands around their necks, as they join the merry parade of cattle and villagers for the climb that means winter is over. The enormous cowbells clang loudly with each ponderous step, but up in the high meadows the sound will come from a distance, thin and silvery.

The men of Appenzell still gather each year in the ancient outdoor town meeting known as the *Landsgemeinde* (LAHNTS-*gay-mine-deh*), where voting is done by a show of hands. Though his elections and his costume belong to another age, this herdsman can bridge the centuries in a matter of moments. All he has to do is go home and exchange the colorful breeches and vest for the drab army uniform hanging in his closet. Presto! The twentieth century!

SOUNDING THE ALPENHORN: LONG-DISTANCE CALL

YOU would think that the last thing a man would want to drag along with him as he climbed the steep mountain pastures was a 15-foot horn. But the rugged Swiss have evidently found this instrument extremely practical for calling the cows home from neighboring peaks, and they are devoted to their monstrous alpenhorns. In fact, their festivals usually include some rousing tunes boomed out in alpenhorn competitions, as well as the milder sounds produced by the human larynx when yodeling.

The alpenhorn can be heard for six miles, and it is really more effective at a distance. The instrument is made from the trunk of a young mountain spruce, and selecting the proper tree is just the first of many problems. The spruce must grow horizontally from a rock crevice and then twist upward. That will give it the natural curve so vital to the foghorn tone the instrument should emit. The curved wood is split, hollowed by hand, then glued together. Sometimes decorations are added to the end, though the player is too far away to see them and presumably his listeners are some miles off, but the artist gets carried away. Ninety working hours after he has plucked his horizontal tree, the artist has an alpenhorn. Sentimental Swiss say that its melancholy groans symbolize a patriotic yearning for the homeland.

The call to civic duty brings all the men to vote at the Landsgemeinde. Schoolboys gather to learn by watching.

53

WHEELS
OF CHEESE:
GOLDEN
STOREHOUSE

FORT Knox with its neatly stacked bars of gold has a great deal in common with this storehouse piled to the rafters with enormous disks of mellow cheese. For the farmers of Switzerland, cheese is the most important and sometimes the only cash crop, and export sales alone can bring in more than twenty million dollars a year.

Cheese is made in many sections of Switzerland and the local products vary in flavor and texture as well as in name. The so-called "Swiss cheese" that Americans like in sandwiches is really Emmentaler (EM-men-tah-lehr), and it comes from the rich Emmental Valley that spreads between Bern and Lucerne. One of the favorite cheeses of Swiss cooks is Gruyère (grew-YEHR), a product of the fine dairy country around Gruyères. But wherever it is made, the process is much the same.

In the summer the village cheese makers move up to the mountain pastures with the cows. There, in a factory that is nothing more than a little hut, each day's supply of milk is poured into a huge caldron that hangs over a log fire. Rennet, a substance that curdles and solidifies milk, is added and stirred and later the thickened mass of curds is placed in round wooden forms. When the cheese starts to ferment it swells into a round shape, and that is why it cannot be forced into a square mold but must be made in wheels. Swiss experts believe that the better the cheese the fewer and smaller the holes. Luckily, there is a good market for the cheeses whose fermentation has not been so carefully controlled.

PEASANT KITCHEN: FARMHOUSE IN THE EMMENTAL

IN RURAL Switzerland food is simple, but hearty and good. Cheese, potatoes and vegetables are served for weekday meals, and on Sundays there is meat. By some standards this might be a rather Spartan diet, but no one seems to be undernourished in Switzerland and children in particular have a healthy bloom.

Two of the best-known regional dishes are fondue (*fohn*-DEW) and *raclette* (*rah*-KLETT), both made with cheese and both involving elements of gamesmanship in their eating. Fondue, a specialty of the French cantons, is a concoction of white wine, Gruyère and Emmental cheese, flavored with garlic and pepper and served bubbling hot in a chafing dish. Each person is given a long fork on which he spears a piece of bread to dip into the gooey cheese. If your bread falls off into the fondue, you have to buy a round of drinks for the other feasters, a punishment for clumsy table manners that no teacher ever thought of. *Raclette* is cheese melted before an open fire right from the wheel. The softened cheese is scraped onto a slice of bread or a boiled potato, and the trick is to twirl your portion on your fork and consume it in one mouthful. No dripping allowed if you want to qualify as a champion *raclette*-eater. Food from country kitchens like this, though inconvenient to prepare, must surely be fun to eat.

This little girl manages to knit, take care of a calf and carry a harvest basket—all at one time, all with a smile.

BORN MOUNTAIN CLIMBER: THE SURE-FOOTED IBEX

HIGH above the valleys where farmhouses nestle, higher even than the Alpine meadows where cows graze in summer, the ibex (EYE-*beks*) roams the craggy peaks of a world where few can venture. These wild goats were once common in the Alps, but the Swiss talents for mountaineering and marksmanship reduced them to near extinction. Then, in 1909, the Swiss League for the Protection of Nature founded a National Park in the Engadine. Now rare Alpine wildlife and flowers flourish there, protected from everything but the hazards of nature.

The ibex lives above the line of perpetual snow, picking its way with astonishing agility over rocky ledges thousands of feet in the sky. At night the small herds climb down to feed in the woods that grow just below the snow line, but daylight finds them clambering back to their dizzy heights, well camouflaged against the tawny stone.

Fortunately for Swiss wildlife, the hunter's horn sounds and his rifle cracks for only a very short season.

The female gives birth to only one baby at a time—what mother could be expected to look after several youngsters at once under these conditions? Remarkably enough, a newborn ibex is able to follow its mother immediately after birth, and one of the wonders of the world must be the sight of a baby ibex tottering up a mountainside on spindly legs. It pays to start young!

58

THE CARD
PLAYERS:
LONG WINTER
PASTIME

WHEN the villages and towns of Switzerland are snugly blanketed with snow, what better way to pass the evenings than at the local inn playing cards. The national card game is called *jass* (YAHSS), and judging from the expressions these men wear it requires a degree of good-natured shrewdness.

The men of Switzerland enjoy their own tightly knit society in a masculine world, and the neighborhood inn or café is their special province. Women do not accompany them for a social evening of cards and talk, nor do they attend any of the numerous civic or political meetings that occupy their husbands. Swiss women do not vote, nor do most of them want to. They even have a society called the Swiss Women's Union Against Votes for Women, in case there are any doubts about their feelings. Men run the country, women rule the home (and, incidentally, spend more than one-third of the national income), and everyone seems happy with that arrangement.

In a country where all men are Army buddies, it is not surprising to find this kind of social life. In the old days the Swiss citizen soldier voted by raising his hand at the *Landsgemeinde,* or outdoor town meeting. And he wore a sword strapped to his side as a sign that he was ready to protect the state of which he was a voting citizen. The double responsibility of sword and ballot persists today. A Swiss man may have to go to the polls as often as fifteen times in the course of a year to vote for officials or to decide on new roads, hospitals, taxes or national defense. The men forgather to discuss the issues before voting, and often, when there is a difference of opinion in the village, a real quarrel blows up and friends stop talking to one another. That is when the female noncombatants step into the picture as peacemakers so that their men can once again enjoy a friendly card game—and get out of the house.

TROUT
FISHERMAN:
SOLITARY SPORT

IN SWITZERLAND there are sports to suit all moods and personalities. For the daring ones who feel the need to pit their puny strength against the mountains, there are the bold challenges of majestic peaks to be climbed. For those who thrill to speed and danger, St.-Moritz offers the breakneck descent of the bobsled run. The naturalist will revel in the protected acres of the National Park where edelweiss blooms shyly on the heights, and ibex and chamois move from mountaintop to mountaintop, perpetual fugitives from the treacherous lowlands. Convivial souls will find their fun racing down the fashionable ski slopes like a flock of birds in flight, to meet afterwards for gay chatter over hot drinks at the lodge.

But for the lover of solitude who enjoys matching his wits against the wily denizens of stream or lake, Switzerland offers supreme opportunities. Long before the Helvetians (*hell*-VEE-*shanz*) and Romans brought their civilizations here, the land was peopled by lake dwellers who lived contentedly in this fishermen's Eden. The clear, cold mountain lakes and crystal rivers were filled with an abundance of fish, and today, thanks to laws that safeguard the rivers from pollution and keep them well-stocked, modern fishermen have it as good as the ancient lake dwellers ever did.

A champion skier zigzags down the course at top speed in a slalom race.

SUSPENSION BRIDGE: TAMING THE ALPS

THE dramatic scenery of Switzerland is the country's greatest glory—and its biggest problem. How, in this era of easy and rapid communication, do you link together a land slashed by deep gorges, cut by innumerable rivers, walled by mountain barriers thousands of feet high? The ingenuity of Swiss engineers has produced some remarkable solutions, and astonishingly enough, while taming the wild splendor, they did not detract from its beauty. The mile upon mile of excellent roads that snake through craggy mountain chains are as breath-taking as the land they are making accessible. And Swiss bridges poised above wicked gorges or arched gracefully over rushing rivers are a thrilling reminder that man's handiwork, too, has elements of grandeur. The Swiss-born engineer Othmar Ammann (AHM-*mahn*) planned the George Washington Bridge and the Lincoln Tunnel in New York. His homeland was an excellent proving ground.

The Swiss railroads look like toy trains, dwarfed as they are by the landscape of titanic cliffs and peaks through which they travel. But building them was far from child's play. They clatter across nearly 5000 bridges and roar through more than 600 tunnels, binding the Swiss cantons together with rails of steel. The Simplon (SIM-*plohn*) Tunnel, largest in the world, carries trains beneath the mountains for a distance of twelve miles. Its mid-point is the Swiss-Italian frontier, and we can traverse in a few easy minutes what Napoleon and his armies struggled to cross when they marched over the Simplon Pass.

As a result of the improved roads and railroads, one picturesque Alpine tradition has virtually disappeared. The famous brandy-toting dogs who used to rescue travelers lost in the snows of the Great St. Bernard Pass have little to do these days. They are usually called upon now only to pose for camera-toting travelers.

LUCERNE:
FIRST CITY
OF THE
CONFEDERATION

THIS graceful old town stands on the shore of the Lake of the Four Forest Cantons—also known as Lake Lucerne—with the River Reuss (ROYCE) cutting a blue path between its buildings. Lucerne has long been a favorite with travelers, but it has such great intrinsic charm that even hordes of tourists do not detract from it.

Situated at Switzerland's heart—both geographically and sentimentally—Lucerne and its three neighboring Forest Cantons were the early nucleus of the Confederation. The oddly shaped lake whose arms reach into the four cantons of Uri (oo-*ree*), Schwyz, Unterwalden (OON-*ter-vahl-den*) and Lucerne, laps at the most historic shores in Switzerland. This is the land of William Tell and the birthplace of Swiss independence. On the green meadow called Rütli, with guardian mountains rising in the background, three Swiss patriots clasped hands and swore the oath that reinforced the Everlasting Pact of 1291.

Lucerne itself is encrusted with history. Parts of the old city walls still stand, their sentinel towers reminding us of the uneasy past. The narrow streets in the old quarter are scarcely wide enough for a single car to pass through, and the buildings are decorated with gaily painted frescoes and hung with old-fashioned signs. Nevertheless, since the Swiss are practical above all, even the most ancient shops display thoroughly modern merchandise. The most distinctive sight in all Lucerne is the old covered bridge that slants across the river. This is the Kapellbrücke (kah-PELL-*brew-keh*), built in the fourteenth century, and under its peaked roof are a series of triangular paintings on wood that depict the history of Switzerland and Lucerne. One writer said, "If I wanted to teach a child or a stranger to understand Switzerland I would not buy him a guidebook, but would take him first to Lucerne and walk him over that bridge whose ancient planks ring under one's step . . ."

THE FACE OF SWITZERLAND: STRENGTH AND DIGNITY

THE face we see here recurs again and again throughout Swiss history. The forceful features half-hidden by a shaggy beard appear in statues of William Tell and in pictures of Arnold von Winkelried (*fonn* VIN-*kel-reet*), the fourteenth-century Swiss hero who breached the Austrian battle line by throwing himself on the enemy lances; we see this stern, strong face in the leaders of the Reformation, and Henri Dunant, founder of the Red Cross, bore a striking resemblance to this man. This is the look typical of many oldsters in Switzerland today, and since a man's face at this age has been shaped by his character, it is a good clue to the national traits that are a heritage from the nation's heroes.

Frugal and simple in their tastes, the Swiss—with their emphasis on quality—make even a meal of bread and milk something delicious. The milk may be still warm and fresh from the family goat. The bread is an honest peasant loaf, firm-textured and nourishing. The bowl and pitcher are examples of Swiss artistry in everyday objects. We see in this peasant a man who is proud of what he is and contented with what he has. There is little more to ask of life.

Dressed in ancestral uniforms, the men of this tiny valley march in a traditional Sunday procession.

69

GOLDEN VINEYARDS: HILLSIDE ABOVE LAKE OF GENEVA

THE blue crescent of the Lake of Geneva lies at the sunny southwestern corner of Switzerland, its upper shore Swiss, its lower shore French. This is the section of Switzerland that is most like France, and you will see the Gallic spirit reflected in the lightheartedness of the people, whose language is French, and in the towns that garland the lake shore—Lausanne, Vevey (*vuh*-VEH), Montreux (*mohn*-TRUH), gayer and more cosmopolitan than most Swiss cities. Lausanne is famous for its university, colleges and fine private schools, and its citizens speak a French that is faultlessly pure.

The hills that face the southern sun are neatly terraced with vineyards whose grapes were probably brought to this region by the Romans. Other cantons may pride themselves on their rich dairy products; the Canton of Vaud (VOH) delights in its flourishing vineyards that produce some of the best wines in Switzerland. Resembling Moselle or Rhine wine, they are light and delicate, but with a high alcoholic content. Every twenty-five years or so the entire countryside turns out in a brilliant festival to honor their vinegrowers. The festival

Near Montreux in October the luscious grapes are harvested, but a few escape the wine barrel.

takes place in Vevey, a short distance from the town of Rivaz (*ree*-VAHZ) which we see in this picture. The pagan god of wine, Bacchus (BACK-*us*), is enthroned during the spectacular two-week ceremonies, and for that brief period the countryside seems to revert to earlier times.

70

GENEVA REFLECTIONS: LAKE FRONT AT NIGHT

THE city of Geneva uses Switzerland's wealth of electricity with a lavish hand, and after dark this staid center of Calvinism blossoms with bright lights. If you look closely, though, you will see that the carnival gaiety is only the result of colored advertising signs. Watchmakers and insurance companies light up the sky and the water, testifying to Geneva's importance as a commercial and financial center. The Rhone River rushes through the city, from the Lake of Geneva on its way to France and the warm Mediterranean. The tree-shaded quays along the waterfront are lively with strollers, and the sound of music drifts out of innumerable cafés.

John Calvin would not have approved. When he lived and preached in Geneva, his discipline was severe. There was to be no running or playing in the streets during the time of the Sunday sermons; women were to forswear certain fashions, including embroidered sleeves; feasts, no matter how important the occasion or how wealthy the host, were not to exceed three courses. But though it was austere, Geneva encouraged the rich, full life of the intellect and opened its doors to freethinking refugees from less liberal lands.

In one of the parks of this "Rome of Protestantism" is the immense Monument of the Reformation. The bas-relief, more than one hundred yards long, bears the carved likenesses of Luther, Zwingli, Calvin, John Knox, Roger Williams, Oliver Cromwell and other leaders of Protestantism. Inscribed in stone, in the language of each man, are the famous statements and guiding principles that have left so deep an imprint upon our culture in the past four hundred years.

Julius Caesar was the first foreign visitor to write about Geneva—he was there in 58 B.C. Since that time this international city has attracted writers and thinkers, convention delegates and just plain tourists from all over the world, who find that the sparkling charm of French-Swiss Geneva has not been completely "reformed."

CASTLE OF CHILLON: ROMANTIC DUNGEON

REFLECTED in the crinkled blue surface of the Lake of Geneva is the fabled Castle of Chillon (*she*-YOHN). The years have mellowed its grim towers, and here, framed by branches of forsythia and warmed by gentle sunlight, the castle has a prettiness quite inconsistent with its history. A jagged rock rises out of the Lake of Geneva not far from Montreux. Men of the Bronze Age lived on the tiny island, and centuries later it was fortified by Caesar's busy legions—probably because the site was strategic for guarding the valleys that led to the Alpine passes.

The Castle as we see it now was built by the Duke of Savoy in the thirteenth century. Two hundred years later its cellar became a "dungeon dark and dank" for Francis Bonivard, prior of an abbey in Geneva, who was imprisoned for his Protestant activities. For six years Bonivard was chained to a pillar in a vault whose barred windows were at water level. Lord Byron visited the castle in 1816 and his poetic imagination,

On the river near the mighty Rhine Falls, the city of Schaffhausen drowses beneath old castle walls.

always fired by causes and romantic settings, invented a more dramatic version of Bonivard's story. The poem *The Prisoner of Chillon* made the castle famous, but in case it would not do as much for him, Byron scratched his name boldly on one of the dungeon pillars.

BERNESE CHALET: HOUSE BEAUTIFUL

IT IS not only the medieval castles in Switzerland that give the country a fairy-tale enchantment. Some of the beautiful old farmhouses and inns look as though they might belong in a storybook by Grimm or Andersen. The fanciful gingerbread architecture of the chalets in the canton of Bern is especially delightful.

The woodcarver's art shows to advantage on the fine old timberwork, and painted designs on the outside of the house add charm and coziness to buildings that have sheltered many generations from Alpine snows. The houses are lovingly cared for and handed down from father to son. It is not unusual to find a wooden chalet that has been in the same family for hundreds of years.

One of the most famous modern architects is the Swiss Charles Edouard Jeanneret (*zhahn*-REH), known to the world as Le Corbusier (*luh kor-bew*-ZYAY). His severe concrete and glass skyscrapers (he helped design the U.N. Secretariat in New York) seem to have little relationship with the buildings of his native land, but Le Corbusier's famous dictum, "the house is a machine for living in," could apply to the Swiss chalet. For it, too, has been thoughtfully engineered. The distinctive roof, steeply pitched, allows the heavy winter snows to melt and slide off easily. The overhanging eaves and balconies that are such charming features of Swiss architecture are protection from the severe winters. These "machines" have functioned well in Switzerland for a long, long time, snugly warm in winter, while in summer, banked with flowers, they express the joyousness of a brighter season.

THE GREAT OUTDOORS: MAGNIFICENT WORLD

INVITING as the houses of Switzerland are, it is the glorious outdoors that beckons to native and visitor alike. In a country where "every prospect pleases," hiking is a great national pastime, and picnicking a favorite pleasure. On roads and mountain paths you encounter groups of young people, ruddy-cheeked from the Alpine sun, husky and fit as a result of fresh air and exercise. With knapsacks on their backs, they walk with the steady, slow pace of the experienced mountaineer, for the Swiss have learned that in their high altitudes "you get there faster if you walk slowly." Furthermore, it gives you time to lift your eyes and contemplate the world of beauty all around you.

The young people in this picture are pausing, but not to catch their breath—though the view is breath-taking. They have stopped to gaze at the ageless miracle of the snowy-crested Matterhorn. How many millions of eyes have taken in this view, how many minds have marveled at it since the earliest lake-dwellers stood mute with wonder at this land that was theirs! The practical Swiss have no need to create poetry, compose symphonies, paint masterpieces. In their country every mountain is a sonnet, every waterfall a concerto, and every landscape a work of art. Their talent lies in their tranquil appreciation of these gifts.

Swiss youngsters climb high above a mountain valley to be rewarded with this splendid panorama of their land.

SOME IMPORTANT DATES IN SWISS HISTORY

58 B.C.	*The Helvetii, a Celtic tribe occupying the area now known as Switzerland, try to emigrate to present-day France but are defeated by Julius Caesar and incorporated into the Roman Empire.*
250-450	*Helvetia (modern-day Switzerland) is invaded by the Alamanni and Burgundians. The Alamanni introduce the Germanic dialect now spoken by most Swiss.*
1033	*Switzerland becomes part of the Holy Roman Empire.*
August 1, 1291	*The alliance of the three cantons of Schwyz, Uri and Unterwalden marks the beginning of the Swiss Confederation.*
1315	*The three cantons defeat the Hapsburgs at the battle of Morgarten and secure independence. Rütli Pact of 1291 is renewed.*
1353	*Confederation expands to a league of eight cantons.*
1499	*Treaty of Basel is signed, granting the Swiss complete independence from the Holy Roman Empire.*
1519	*The Reformation, under the leadership of Ulrich Zwingli of Zurich, threatens to split the league.*
1648	*Treaty of Westphalia guarantees Switzerland's independence from Germany.*
1798	*France invades Switzerland, sets up Helvetian Republic.*
1803-1813	*Acting as Mediator of Switzerland, Napoleon enlarges the Confederation, bringing the total number of cantons included to nineteen.*
1815	*Congress of Vienna re-establishes Swiss independence. Confederation is made up of twenty-two cantons, as it is today. Perpetual neutrality guaranteed by Peace of Paris.*
1848	*Switzerland adopts a federal constitution. Bern becomes capital of the modern Swiss nation.*
1864	*International Red Cross founded at Geneva.*
1914-1918	*World War I. Switzerland remains neutral. Thousands of prisoners of war and wounded soldiers interned there.*
1920	*League of Nations accepts Switzerland as a neutral member state. Geneva is designated headquarters of the League.*
1939-1945	*World War II. General Henri Guisan heads Swiss forces, keeps Switzerland from being invaded by Hitler. Humanitarian work of country continues.*
1949	*Geneva becomes the permanent home of the United Nations World Health Organization (WHO).*

SOME FAMOUS NAMES IN SWISS HISTORY

ST. GALLUS (550?-645?)—*Irish missionary to Switzerland. In 613 he founded the celebrated monastery of St. Gallen.*

ST. BERNARD OF MENTHON (923-1008)—*Roman Catholic priest, protector of Alpine climbers. In 962, he founded the famous hospices for lost wayfarers.*

WILLIAM TELL (14th century)—*National hero of Switzerland. Semi-legendary patriot who was forced by Austrian oppressor to shoot an apple off his son's head.*

ARNOLD VON WINKELRIED (14th century)—*In 1386 at the battle of Sempach he threw himself on the Austrian lances, enabling Swiss forces to breach the line and fight on to victory.*

ULRICH ZWINGLI (1484-1531)—*Religious reformer. Established Reformation in Zurich, legalized by council of Zurich in 1523.*

PARACELSUS (1493?-1541)—*Physician and alchemist. Persecuted for advocating scientific observation rather than tradition.*

JOHN CALVIN (1509-1564)—*French theologian. Banished from his native land, he established a theocratic government at Geneva, which became a stronghold of the Reformation.*

JEAN JACQUES ROUSSEAU (1712-1778)—*Philosopher, musician, novelist, and diarist. His writings exerted profound influence on education and political thought in the 18th century.*

JOHANN HEINRICH PESTALOZZI (1746-1827)—*Educational reformer and humanitarian, called the "Father of Swiss Education." Influenced instruction methods in elementary schools throughout Europe and America.*

JOHANNA SPYRI (1827-1901)—*Writer of children's books, including the classic Heidi.*

JEAN HENRI DUNANT (1828-1910)—*Philanthropist. In 1864 he established the International Red Cross, for which he won the Nobel Peace Prize in 1901.*

CESAR RITZ (1850-1918)—*Hotelkeeper and restaurateur.*

HENRI GUISAN (1874-1960)—*General whose bold and decisive diplomacy during World War II discouraged the Germans from invading Switzerland and preserved Swiss neutrality.*

CARL JUNG (1875-1961)—*Psychiatrist and founder of analytic psychology.*

PAUL KLEE (1879-1940)—*Modernist painter with an individual style of expressing the subconscious mind and phantasy in art.*

LE CORBUSIER (*Pseudonym of Charles Edouard Jeanneret, 1887-   )—Architect, painter and writer. Pioneer in creating modern functional architecture.*

ARTHUR HONEGGER (1892-1955)—*Composer. Among his works are the oratorios* King David *and* Nicholas de Flue, *and the Biblical drama* Judith.

SOME WORDS AND PHRASES FOR SWITZERLAND

Here is a list of words and phrases which would be useful for any visitor to Switzerland. The Swiss are multilingual, and many of them speak English. But the two languages most used are German and French.

ENGLISH	GERMAN	FRENCH
Do you speak English?	Sprechen Sie english? SHPREH-*khen zee* EN-*glish?*	Parlez-vous anglais? *pahr-leh-voo zawn-*GLEH?
I do not understand.	Ich verstehe nicht *ikh fehr-*SHTEH-*heh nikht*	Je ne comprends pas *zhuh nuh kohm-prawn pah*
Excuse me.	Pardon *pahr-*DOHN	Pardon *pahr-dohng*
Please.	Bitte BIT-*teh*	S'il vous plaît *seel voo pleh*
Thank you (very much).	Danke (sehr) DAHN-*keh zehr*	Merci (beaucoup) *mehr-see boh-koo*
Hello. Good-bye.	Guten Tag Adieu GOO-*ten tahk* *ah-*D'YUH	Bonjour Adieu *bohn-*ZHOOR *ah-*D'YUH
Where is . . . ? How far?	Wo ist . . . ? Wie weit? *voh isst . . . ? vee vite?*	Où est . . . ? A quelle distance? *oo-eh . . . ? ah-kehl-dees-*TAWNSS?
How much does it cost?	Was kostet das? *vah* KOHS-*tett dahs?*	Combien coûte cela? *kohm-b'yehn koot suh-*LAH?
I wish to purchase . . .	Ich brauche . . . *ikh* BROW-*kheh . . .*	Je désire acheter . . . *zhuh deh-zeer ahsh-teh . . .*
Watch	Uhr OOR	montre MOHNTR'
Typewriter	Schreibmaschine SHRIBE-*mah-shee-neh*	machine à écrire *mah-sheen ah eh-*KREER
Guide	Führer FEW-*rehr*	guide GEED
Mountain	Berg BEHRK	montagne *mohn-tahn-yuh*
Lake	See ZEH	lac LAHK
Valley	Tal TAHL	vallée *vah-*LEH
Road	Strasse SHTRAH-*seh*	route ROOT
Food	Essen ESS-*s'n*	de quoi manger *duh kwah mawn-*ZHEH
Drink	Trinken TRIN-*k'n*	de quoi boire *duh kwah* BWAHR
Store	Geschäft *geh-*SHEFFT	magasin *mah-gah-*ZEHNG
Today	heute HOY-*teh*	aujourd'hui *oh-zhoor-*DWEE
Tomorrow	morgen MOHR-*g'n*	demain *duh-*MEHNG
Ladies' room	Damentoilette DAH-*men-twah-let-teh*	Dames DAHM
Mens' room	Herrentoilette HER-*rehn-twah-let-teh*	Messieurs *meh-s'yuh*
Airport	Flughafen FLOOK-*hah-f'n*	aéroport *ah-eh-roh-*POHR
Railway station	Bahnhof BAHN-*hohf*	gare GAR
Boat	Schiff SHIFF	bateau *bah-toh*

INDEX